Old Blyth
John Alexander

Rebecca Todd's china and glassware shop in Blagdon Street was stocked with a rich variety of goods.

© John Alexander, 2015
First published in the United Kingdom, 2015,
by Stenlake Publishing Ltd.
www.stenlake.co.uk
ISBN 9781840337167

Acknowledgements

I am very grateful to George Nairn whose generous contribution of pictures and stories made the compilation of this book possible. I must also thank the Beamish Photographic Archive for permission to use the pictures on pages 3, 9, 12, 13, 16, 28 and 36. The resources of Northumberland Libraries, especially those of Blyth Library were invaluable. Websites, too numerous to list, also proved to be important as a source of information, while the friendliness of local people made the task of piecing stories together easier and at the same time more pleasurable.

Further Reading

Atkinson, Constance; Butters, Peter; Durward, Dave and Routledge, Elder; *Blyth Then and Now*, 1999.
Blyth Local Studies Group, *Blyth*, reprinted 2011.
Kirkup, Mike, *Ashington Coal Company; the Five Collieries*, 2000.
Linsley, Stafford, *Ports and Harbours of Northumberland*, 2005.
National Coal Board, *Coal (magazine)*, Sept. 1948 & Feb. 1952.
Prins, Stanley (Editor), *A Guide to the Anglican Churches in Newcastle upon Tyne and Northumberland*, 1982.
Company History: *The Ashington Coal Company Ltd.*, 1912.

Cowpen Village (*upper*), which gave its name to the early colliery developments in the area and Monkey Island (*lower*), a playground for youngsters until industry took over.

Introduction

When Blyth gained its Royal Charter in 1922 it adopted the motto 'We Grow by Industry', which was not just aspirational, it was also a good description of how the burgh had got to where it was. The Blyth name was initially just that of the river, which provided shelter for boats, but it was a difficult harbour to get in and out of, so activity was limited. Although natural forces restricted shipping, they conversely provided outcropping coal and seawater, the main ingredients of a thriving salt industry. Fishing, an occupation that benefitted from a ready supply of salt, was another early industry, but while these activities were destined to decline, another grew in their place: coal mining.

At first the collieries were situated at a distance from the river mouth, but as rail transport developed and pits proliferated across the rich Northumberland coalfield the need for improved shipping facilities became a practical and economic necessity. Surrounded by pits, the River Blyth might have seemed pre-destined to become a major coaling port, but with inadequate infrastructure and navigational restrictions nothing was certain. Control by private owners passed to the Blyth Harbour and Docks Board in 1854 and some improvements were made, but constrained financially the Board was unable fully to capitalise on the river's location. That changed and the port began to achieve its potential when the harbour's management and development was taken over by the Blyth Harbour Commissioners in 1882.

While the river was inching and then accelerating towards prosperity, the villages and settlements on its south side were growing together as a town. A centre developed around the market place with churches, shops, public buildings and places of entertainment putting down roots. For recreation, people could head for the superb beach, but a fine public park was added to the urban mix and sporting activities grew, notably a football team with a name feared in ancient Greece and modern England alike.

The river developed in other ways with shipbuilding, ship breaking and fishing industries added to the coal trade that grew inexorably until 1961 when record shipments briefly made Blyth the busiest coal exporting port in Europe. The building of a power station gave the town a new, if short-lived landmark and for a time the aluminium industry had a presence on the waterfront, but the peak had been passed and as the coal industry's painful decline gathered pace, Blyth's fortunes waned. The loss of exports saw the demise of the staithes, but not to be forgotten these great structures that once resounded to rumbling wagons and tumbling coal were commemorated by the *Spirit of the Staithes*, a spectacular piece of public art unveiled in May 2003.

As with many communities affected by the loss of major industries the town is reinventing itself. The beach and its restored wartime defences draw tourists, transport links are being improved and the harbour remains a haven for big ships and small boats. Situated on a beautiful coast close to a great city, it is in a good place and the warm friendly people make it a good place to be in.

An advertisement for T. D. Redhead's Star Confectionery Works.

Blyth was a tricky port to get in and out of in a sailing ship, especially when the sea was running in an onshore wind. Improvements to the navigation were made only gradually, with the rocks on the east side of the channel forming a base for a breakwater and pier that eventually extended for about a mile and was finished off with a lighthouse. The west side of the channel was also protected by a pier and marked by the navigation light seen here. With the channel properly confined by the piers the sand bar, which restricted the harbour entrance, could be dredged successfully. Prior to that the depth of water at the bar could at certain states of the tide be down to only a few feet while paradoxically there was deeper water inside the harbour. Steam ships began to replace the sailing colliers in the late 19th century, but as this picture from 1906 shows some sailing vessels continued to use the harbour. The one shown here is leaving the port with the assistance of a tug and with the pilot boat in attendance to ensure the ship cleared the port safely.

It wasn't just sailing vessels that needed assistance from tugs to navigate the narrow harbour entrance, as this picture of a steam collier under tow shows. The early sailing vessels plying the east coast were little more than barges, like Humber keels. By the mid 18th century these had evolved into broad-beamed bluff-ended barks epitomised by the Whitby collier, the kind of vessels chosen by Captain James Cook, a Whitby man, for his voyages of discovery describing them as 'north-country-built ships . . . for the coal trade'. A gradual change from these three-masted barks to two-masted 'Geordie' collier-brigs had taken place by the mid 19th century when steam-powered vessels began to appear. Initially the transition was slow, but accelerated as machinery design improved. By 1894 when the steam turbine was developed the steam to sail ratio had reached three to one. The steam collier, with its 'salt-caked smoke stack', had completely superseded its sailing predecessors by the 1920s or early 1930s when this picture was taken.

Of the many tugs that assisted shipping in and out of Blyth Harbour the one with arguably the most distinctive name was the *Earl of Beaconsfield*, seen here shortly before she was scrapped in 1913. It's a curious name because the title, the *Earl of Beaconsfield*, was created for Tory Prime Minister Benjamin Disraeli in 1876; perhaps somebody enjoyed the irony of a tug, so-named, being put to work serving the needs of the coal industry. The tug was built by J. P. Rennoldson of South Shields in 1877, the year after Disraeli's ennoblement, and came to Blyth ten years later. The Blyth Steam Tug Company appear to have liked the name because in 1922 they bought another paddle tug, the *Salt*, and renamed her *Earl of Beaconsfield*. Unlike her wooden-hulled predecessor, she had a steel hull and had been built by J. T. Eltringham of South Shields in 1889. She was scrapped at North Blyth ship breakers Hughes Bolckow in 1958. The other tugs working at Blyth tended to have less ostentatious names like *Greatham*, *Langton*, *Seasider* or *Steel*.

The names given to the Blyth Harbour Commissioners' dredgers reflected the local area. There was the *Cambois*, introduced in 1895, a bucket dredger built by Fleming and Ferguson at Paisley on the River Cart, a tributary of the Clyde. She was replaced by the vessel seen in this picture, the *Cowpen*, a twin screw, stern-well bucket hopper dredger built by Ferguson Brothers, specialists in fabricating this type of craft. Their yard at Port Glasgow on the lower Clyde occupied a site cheek by jowl with the 15th century Newark Castle, a remarkable historical survivor given that it was once all but surrounded by shipyards. *Cowpen* arrived at Blyth in 1913 and remained as a feature of harbour life until 1964. With debris deposited by the river, and wind-blown tides driving in sand, the harbour was prone to silting up and needed constant dredging to maintain an adequate working depth. Rocky intrusions on the riverbed were also a hazard and a combination of explosives and a boat with a vertically mounted battering ram was used to break up the rock, which was then cleared away by the dredger.

Blyth developed as a port for the handling of one principal cargo, coal. Instead therefore of wharves, cranes and dockside sheds, its waterfront was lined with a variety of staithes, structures designed to receive railway trucks full of coal at a level, which at the highest tide was higher than ships riding high with empty holds. The trucks could then be tipped and gravity did the rest as the coal was shot down chutes into the waiting collier, in a cloud of black dust. On the left of this picture looking upstream, are the North Eastern Railway's South Blyth Staithes, which reached a peak of development in the late 19th century and closed in the 1960s. The staithes on the right were built for the Cowpen Coal Company to load coal from their Cambois Colliery. They were originally erected in the 1860s, modified in the 1890s to accommodate harbour improvements and closed in 1968. In the following decade a terminal for the import of bauxite was built on the site. From there, using the existing rail connection, the mineral was taken to a new aluminium smelter at Lynemouth. The smelter closed in 2012.

The railway line serving the Cowpen staithes in the picture on the facing page ran along the shore and then swung through a 90° curve to head straight out to the loading end of the structure. Just upstream of the Cowpen staithes was the North Eastern Railway Company's remarkable North Side Staithes, seen here in the early 1920s. A long sinuous structure, it was built with the railway tracks running along the top so that ships could be loaded at a number of berths at the same time. It was opened in 1896 to ship coal, principally from the Ashington Coal Company's collieries located to the north of Blyth. Development of the coalfield began in the 1860s and by the time this picture was taken the group comprised Ashington, Woodhorn, Linton and Ellington collieries; Lynemouth was added a few years later. With the exception of Linton the pits were all still working in the early 1970s when the staithes were closed and demolished to wharf level. The little harbour passenger ferry can be seen tootling across the river in front of the staithes.

With a slipway at North Blyth and another beside the Golden Fleece Inn at Cowpen Square, a vehicular ferry began hauling itself across the river in 1890, taking over from an earlier ferry. The ferry ceased to operate in 1964 following the opening of the Kitty Brewster Bridge. As is clear from this picture of Ferry No. 2, it was cable operated. Cable (or earlier chain) ferries were once quite common, especially at crossings where the boat was subject to river or tidal flows, as at Blyth. They worked by having cables attached to both sides of the crossing that also passed through the boat and were long enough to sink to the bottom once the ferry had passed. The boat's engine hauled the cable through pulley wheels that gave it traction depending on the direction the boat was travelling. The cabins on either side of the boat enclosed the engines and were also used for passenger accommodation, while vehicles sat in the centre balancing the boat. Behind the ferry on the right of this picture, which was used as a postcard in 1923, are the North Blyth Staithes.

The most conveniently located pit for its loading point was Bates Colliery. It was situated adjacent to the two conveyor loaders that can be seen beyond the foreground jetty on the left of a picture that was probably taken in the early 1930s, soon after the construction of these dramatic-looking structures. They were erected by F. Turnbull of Heaton, and fed coal by way of conveyors that could be swung through an arc and adjusted in height and reach to shoot the cargo into a ship's holds from no great height, without the vessel having to be moved. They could handle up to 400 tons of coal an hour. In the background, in the centre of the picture, are the West Staithes constructed jointly by the Harbour Commissioners and the North Eastern Railway and completed in 1926. Jutting straight out from the Cambois shore into the West Basin, a lagoon formed by the confluence of the River Blyth and the Sleek Burn the staithes were an impressive structure. They were demolished in the mid 1990s. The shelving beach and small boats in the foreground show that the river wasn't given over solely to large ships and industry.

Much of the coal shipped from the River Blyth in the 16th and 17th centuries had come from mines situated a few miles away, but in 1794 the Cowpen 'A' shaft was sunk in the immediate vicinity of the developing town. A second 'B' shaft followed soon after the first, and although there had been early rivalry between the Cowpen developers and local land-owning entrepreneur Sir Matthew Ridley, that was soon healed and the pits and harbour began to grow. Another new shaft, the Isabella, was sunk in the mid 19th century and in 1885 Crofton Mill Pit, usually known simply as the Mill, was opened. These pits were showing signs of age by the late 1920s when the Cowpen Coal Company's director and engineer Sidney Bates began an extensive reconstruction scheme. He also initiated a new sinking close to the river at 'Monkey Island' in 1932. Bates Pit as it became known, is seen here in 1936 with the large coal preparation plant and Baum washer prominent behind the headgear; it was company policy to deliver washed coal of uniform size to customers.

The British coal industry was nationalised on 1st January 1947 and by the early 1950s plans were being drawn up for a major reconstruction of Bates Pit, which only 20 years earlier had been regarded as fully modern. The plans also included the Mill and Isabella Pits. A major element of the scheme was a level locomotive haulage road to the sub-sea Beaumont seam workings and, with the Plessey seam linked by conveyor to a loading point, output was expected to increase fivefold. Coal would be moved in large-capacity mine cars, instead of tubs, and wound to the surface in a new, deeper shaft. At the end of it all, Bates was a more up-to-date pit than it appears in this picture from 1957. Although equipped with battery lamps, two of the men are still wearing cloth caps designed to support the old style carbide lamps. It is not clear if they were working on development or a face line that has yet to be mechanised, but the roof has been well supported with Dowty hydraulic props. Reductions in pit numbers in the 1960s saw the closure of the Isabella Pit in 1966 and Crofton Mill in 1969, but Bates remained in operation until it was closed in May 1986.

The Cowpen Coal Company also operated a pit to the north of the river at Cambois and another north of the River Wansbeck at North Seaton, both opened in the mid 19th century. The picture shows the houses of Wembley Terrace at Cambois where many mining families lived. Cambois worked the Low Main, Plessey and Yard seams and also extracted fireclay. Later the pit went on to work the Five Quarter and Bensham seams. At the time of the Bates sinking, the company built a new screening and washing plant at Cambois, and laid a narrow gauge railway, with a bridge across the River Wansbeck, to take tubs of coal from North Seaton to the new plant. Treated coal from both pits could then be taken by rail to the staithes at North Blyth. And it wasn't just the coal that got washed, the men of both pits voted to have pithead baths installed in 1936. North Seaton closed in 1961 and Cambois in 1968, but one of the pulley wheels from the headgear was saved for posterity and placed at the entrance to the QEII Silver Jubilee Park, created out of the colliery waste heaps at Ashington.

The Seven Stars Inn was a watering hole on the southern end of the spit of land between the river and sea at North Blyth. It is seen here in a picture from around 1900 or earlier. The pub was popular with seamen on ships berthed on the east side of the river and fishermen liked to drop in while trying their luck from the adjacent jetty. The Seven Stars is a popular English pub name, although its origins are unclear. Most probably it comes from the Bible, the Book of Revelations, where the seven stars are thought to refer to messengers rather than celestial bodies. The poet, W. H. Auden, placed them in the heavens when he wrote '*I'll love you dear, I'll love you, Till . . . the seven stars go squawking like geese across the sky*'. Such a sentiment, and indeed such a vision, may have occurred to mellow customers, some may even have got religion, although more likely, with serious drinking to be done few will have cared where the name came from. There will have been greater consternation when the pub closed in the 1960s.

The harbour skyline was dramatically altered in the late 1950s when Blyth A Power Station was erected. The building is seen here in the latter stages of construction, with the turbine hall on the left, the 157 feet high boiler house to its right with the 450 feet high chimneys alongside. Situated on the Cambois side of the river, almost opposite the Bates loading point, it was fully commissioned by June 1960. Six years later the neighbouring Blyth B Power Station was brought on stream. It was larger than the A station with chimneys 100 feet taller. The power stations were a mixed blessing, providing employment and an outlet for locally-mined coal, but that coal might otherwise have been shipped from the port. Tens of thousands of tons were burned by the stations every week, with so-called merry-go-round trains of hopper wagons delivering 1,100 tons an hour to the stockpiles. Decommissioned by the year 2000, the stations' demolition did not signal the end of Blyth as an electricity provider because nine wind turbines had been set along the East Pier in the early 1990s and with others located offshore, and a planned programme of replacement, Blyth is likely to be doing its bit for electricity generation for some time.

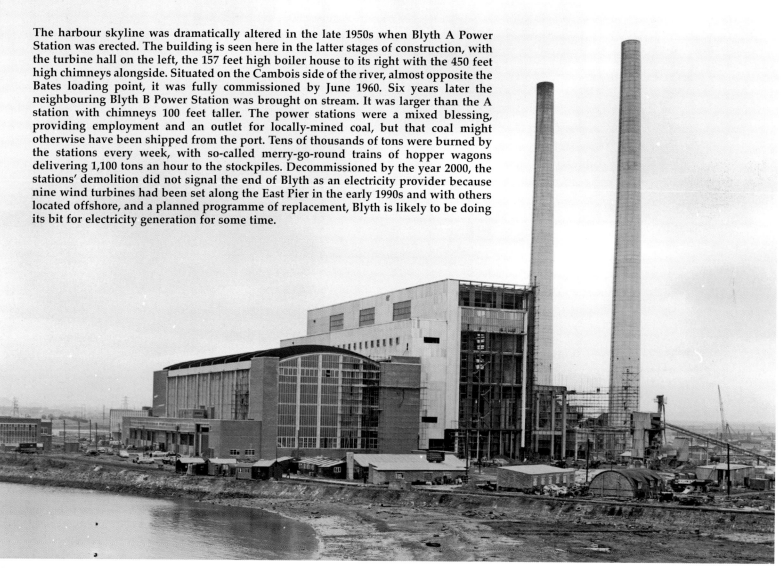

Boats built to the order of The Admiralty, by the Blyth Boat Building Co.

Reading from left to right: 5 Boats for H.M.S. Queen Mary, the remainder to H.M. Dockyard, Sheerness.

South Harbour, Blyth, Northumberland

At the end of the 19th century, when the entrance to the river was widened and deepened, the new South Harbour was created, just inside the main harbour entrance. Opened in 1899 it extended to 23 acres and was connected to the railway network. Ships waiting for a berth at the staithes could lie in the harbour; it was used as a submarine base during the two world wars and also served as the headquarters of the Royal Northumberland Yacht Club. It was lined with conventional wharves and cranes, to handle general cargo, like the pit props seen in the foreground of this picture, which has evidently been used by the Blyth Boat Building Company to advertise a completed Admiralty order. Blyth's main shipbuilding industry was based at Cowpen Quay, but ships were not just built at Blyth; they were broken too at the Hughes Bolckow Shipbreaking Company's yard, which was situated on the north side of the river and gloried in the address of Battleship Wharf. The company also developed an unusual sideline: making garden furniture and furnishings out of the teak salvaged from broken-up warships.

Although never on the scale of great east coast ports like Grimsby or Great Yarmouth, Blyth did have a fishing industry as this picture of herring packers shows. It is popularly thought that the 'shoals of herring' started at one point on the coast and migrated round the British Isles through the season, but later studies showed that separate shoals appeared at different favoured places for spawning. Although the fish may not have migrated, the people did and these fisher lassies and men most probably came from Scotland. At the start of every season, which for Blyth could last from April to September, a small army of people arrived, including the coopers who made the barrels and the men who lifted and loaded them. The fisher lassies, many of them Gaelic-speaking Hebridean islanders, moved with the boats, first to the north-east of Scotland and then on down the east coast to Blyth and other ports. When the herring were landed, the women, standing at large troughs known as farlanes, gutted them with astonishing speed. They then packed them with salt ready for export, in barrels bound with wooden hoops.

The fish market, seen here in a picture used as a postcard in 1914, was in the South Harbour. The boats are all steam drifters, with the one in the foreground showing the registration letters SN for Shields North. The British White Herring Act of 1860 laid down the legal requirement to display these letters and an identifying number. They had to be clearly shown on the boat's bow and sail, and later on the funnels of steam powered boats. Some ports were identified with a single letter, like H for Hull, most used the first and last letters, Blyth was BH, but others were not so obvious like SN and the even trickier SSS for Shields South. Attempts to promote Blyth as a major fishing port in the late 19th century came to naught, although boats still used the harbour and in 1912 another attempt to develop the industry was made when the Port of Blyth Steam Fishing Company was set up. The timing wasn't great, within a couple of years the country was at war and the company's assets were requisitioned. The industry was unable to recover after the war.

The market place for commodities other than fish was in the centre of town at a location where development began about 1815 and took its name from a slightly more famous event that took place at the same time, Waterloo. It is seen here, crowded with stalls, in a picture that can be dated by the movies being screened at the Central Cinema. *The Splendid Road*, a story about women during the California Gold Rush, was made in 1925, while *The Sign of the Claw* starred Peter the Great, the 'Miracle Dog of the Movies' (eat your heart out Lassie) and was doing the rounds in 1926. The Central Cinema opened in December 1924, replacing the earlier Central Hall, which had been built in the 1850s, but was destroyed by fire in 1923: a dramatic event with flames shooting skywards to light up the area following the collapse of the roof. The Central was one of four cinemas in Blyth and could hold over 1,000 patrons, some of whom availed themselves of seats designed for courting couples. It closed in 1961 and became a bingo club, but was demolished in 1974 to allow for redevelopment.

The market place is seen here in 1953, in a similar view to the one on the facing page. Showing at the Central is *Sea Devils*, a forgettable movie set during the Napoleonic Wars (quite appropriate for a location known as Waterloo) starring Rock Hudson and Yvonne De Carlo. Clearly not taken on a market day, the picture is nonetheless interesting because of the presence of the F. W. Woolworth store in place of the buildings formerly occupying Market Street. 'Woolies' was a key element of the town centre shopping area and its loss, when it closed on 5th January 2009, was much lamented. In the same year a scheme to revamp the area was completed. Designed to improve the look of the market, it consisted of new paving, planters, seating and a water feature, all of which in other guises formerly graced the market place. As the picture shows the space in front of the Central Cinema was once laid out with planting and seating, although a drinking fountain, donated by John Hedley, had been removed. The one constant throughout all this change has been Blyth Market.

Horton became a separate parish in 1768 when it was detached from the much larger Woodhorn Parish, but as the population of Blyth began to grow the need arose for a church to serve their needs. Known as a Chapel of Ease, because it eased pressure on the main parish church, St. Mary's Church was built at the northwest corner of Market Place to the designs of Newcastle-based architects Thomas Austin and Robert James Johnson. It consisted of a chancel, nave and south porch and was consecrated in 1864. When it became the parish church in 1897, work began on a new north aisle and extensions to the chancel and west end, all designed by William Searle Hicks. The picture is of uncertain date, but was taken before the Second World War and so omits the large wooden crucifix that was salvaged from a bombed London Church and re-erected outside St. Mary's. Some fine windows have also been installed since the war, in 1950 and 2001.

Church Street, which takes its name from St. Mary's and runs north from Market Place, is seen here in a (slightly blurred) picture that was used as a postcard in 1913. The station can be seen at the far end of the street, but the sender of the card appears to have used another form of transport to meet up with a friend from Glanton. The message on the reverse reads: *'This is the street we live in – No. 61. Got home safe in two and half hours. Hope you got safe back and got no punctures as I had none but nearly run into a hedge when turning a sharp corner; just got my brake on in time.'* It is of course conjecture, but the writer appears to be recounting a journey on a bicycle, an activity that rapidly gained in popularity following John Boyd Dunlop's invention of the pneumatic tyre in 1888. A local club was active in Blyth by the 1890s with the so-called 'wheelmen' meeting at the Railway Hotel before setting off for tours of the local area. The 'season' started at Easter with cyclists (male and female) from Newcastle joining those from Blyth and other places to fill the roads.

Restrictions on the building of Catholic churches were removed by emancipation acts passed by Parliament in the early decades of the 19th century. This provided an opportunity for Catholic architects to make a name for themselves by designing the many new churches that were erected throughout the country. The most famous of these was Augustus Pugin and his sons, but in the north east of England, partners Edward Joseph Hansom and Archibald Matthias Dunn were the foremost Catholic architects and it was the latter who designed the church of Our Lady and St. Wilfrid at the west end of Waterloo Road, at its junction with Edward Street. It was erected in 1861/62, one of many churches built in Blyth to cater for the growing population of industrial workers. The variety of backgrounds from which people came was reflected in the number of different churches and Waterloo Road was a favoured location for some of these. There was an English Presbyterian church opposite Our Lady and St. Wilfrid and churches reflecting two strands of Methodism at the east end of the road.

Blyth's first carnival was held on 3rd September 1924 and the event continued annually up to 1938. That first event also incorporated the opening of a new fire station in Union Street and the formal acquisition by the Burgh Council of the Links, where a programme of dancing, music and sports was held. The great event of that and subsequent carnivals was the parade, seen here with bands, floats and people in fancy dress passing down Waterloo Road. The whole town entered into the spirit of the occasion, streets were adorned in flags and bunting, and shopkeepers decorated their windows. The carnival was also used to raise funds for the Thomas Knight Memorial Hospital in Beaconsfield Street. Opened in 1887 and named after a local ship owner it was a cottage hospital set up through public subscription and endowed with a private bequest, but maintaining such an institution was often a struggle in the days before the NHS. The funds raised by the carnival were therefore of great value, but war intervened in 1939 and the NHS was set up in 1948, obviating the need for large fund raising events. Since then a new community hospital has been built on former railway property.

Just before midnight on 15th October 1904 fire was discovered in a building in Waterloo Road. The fire brigade arrived some 45 minutes after midnight on the morning of the 16th. The hose burst and instead of actually fighting the flames the firemen began by wrestling with their equipment and so by the time they started pumping water the fire had a firm grip. It started in a shop where a waxwork exhibition was being held; the models melted and as the blaze spread it affected neighbouring shops, businesses and residential property. The police had a busy night dealing with looters, controlling the crowds and stopping people from getting in the way of the firemen. One constable, eschewing the modern taste for health and safety, tied a wet handkerchief round his mouth and entered a burning building to rescue a woman and child stranded at the top of a stair. A cat also had a miraculous escape, blown out of a second storey window it landed on its feet, frightened but with eight lives still intact. It was one of Blyth's worst fires destroying nine businesses, four offices and a number of homes.

Instead of expanding from a single core village, as many places did, Blyth was made up of small communities that developed through industrial activity and in spreading out coalesced as a town. The settlement that formed the locus for the town centre also gave its name to the main shopping street, Waterloo Road. It is seen here looking very quiet in a picture taken after the buildings damaged in the 1904 fire had been repaired or replaced. The fire was halted before it reached the Globe Hotel, in the taller of the two buildings on the right with Dutch gable frontages, although there was some water damage. The adjacent building with a Dutch gable, which also escaped the fire, is seen here when occupied by picture framer Thomas H. Teasdale who also dealt in china and glassware. The building on the other side of the Globe remained standing, but was badly damaged by fire and water, while the White Swan pub on the ground floor was looted during the blaze. Unaffected by the fire, the buildings on the left were demolished in more modern times to open up Waterloo Road as one side of the market place.

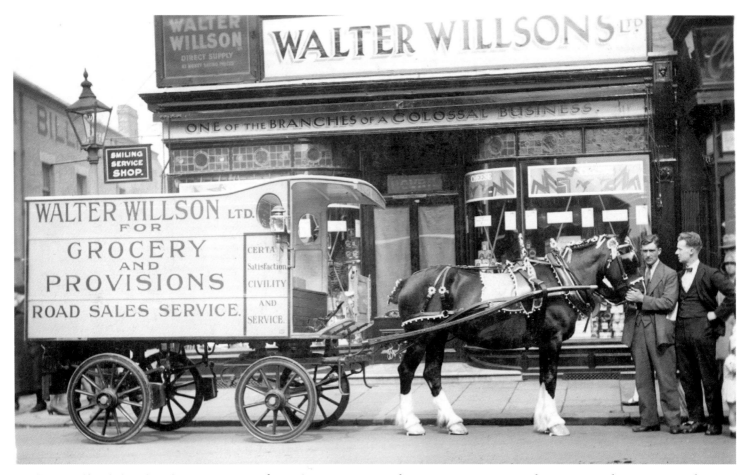

Walter Willson's self-styled 'Colossal Business' was a chain of grocery stores with a presence in many northeast towns. There were two shops in Blyth, this one at the east end of Waterloo Road and a smaller branch at Cowpen Quay. The company appears also to have had a travelling shop although this beautifully turned out horse-drawn van was more likely destined for a parade than a working day. Both the van and the shop are adorned with catchy slogans. These are clearly aimed at attracting customers, but with the use of words like 'smiling' and 'civility' they point to a more personal retail experience than is common in the modern world. Walter Willson's 'smiling service shop' sign and a gas street lamp on the left of the picture partly obscure the end of Trotter Street and a building used as a billiard hall. Known also as the Alexandra Hall it was formerly the Theatre Royal, where Arthur Jefferson, the father of film comedian Stan Laurel, of Laurel and Hardy fame, was an actor manager. During his time, the theatre was rebuilt on a new site, on the corner of Trotter and Jefferson Streets.

The shop occupied by Walter Willson's colossal business was taken down to make way for the Keel Row shopping centre, which was opened in 1991. Many other buildings were demolished in the process, including the Methodist Chapel, which was built in 1869 and dominates the central background of this picture taken in 1938. A new Methodist Chapel was built in Beaconsfield Road to replace it. Methodism, the form of bible study and worship established by John Wesley, his brother Charles and George Whitfield, with its emphasis on ethical values, gained a strong following in industrial communities like Blyth. The bus station in the foreground, has since been modified with the small pavilion and radiating plots being replaced by a much larger building, trees in planters and seats. The vehicle in the background appears to be a red and cream 'United' bus. The company, United Automobile Services, was formed in 1912 and expanded into many parts of England including Northumberland. At the time the picture was taken it was part owned by the London and North Eastern Railway Company.

Blyth Railway Station was made up of a single island platform with a canopy and the terminal building seen in this picture. Situated at the north end of Turner Street, this was not the station's original location having been initially sited further east, on Croft Street (later renamed King Street), close to the later gas works. It was moved in 1867 and then rebuilt in the 1890s to cope with the volume of passengers. Blyth's growth was dependent as much on the railway as it was on shipping coal. Initially it was difficult, verging on the impossible, for the mining industry to expand when horse-drawn carts were the only way of getting coal from the pits to the ships. The position improved with the growth of waggon ways, but the development of railways and, in particular, steam locomotives unlocked the potential of the northeast coalfield. The railway that eventually served Blyth began with a line that was opened for coal traffic between Seghill and staithes on the Tyne at Percy Main in 1840.

In October 1904, ten days after the fire that did so much damage in Waterloo Road (page 26), Cowpen and Blyth District Councils convened to hear a report from the Fire Brigade Superintendent. While the meeting was in progress smoke was seen billowing from Wallace's drapery shop in Turner Street, directly opposite the station, and the fire brigade was once again in action. In another remarkable coincidence a Mr. Elliot, a representative of Shand and Mason, makers of the fire engine, arrived by train half-an-hour before the outbreak occurred. Still clad in his business clothes and wearing a top hat he took charge of the engine and gave a practical demonstration of its capabilities. Despite his expertise, the fire spread quickly into the furniture warehouse and showroom of J. W. Chisholm on one side, the Maypole Dairy on the other and a hairdresser's shop. It also scorched the paintwork of the Blyth and Tyne Hotel. The crowd in the foreground of this picture are surveying the damage from the station entrance, but J. W. Chisholm didn't allow the site to remain a blackened ruin for long, quickly replacing it with a rebuilt 'White Shop'.

The Railway Hotel is on the left of this picture looking south along Turner Street, and beyond that is the White Shop, J. W. Chisholm's extensive furniture emporium, which also sold other useful items like prams and bicycles. Across the road, on the right, is the station forecourt. In 1846 the railway between Percy Main and Seghill was extended north to Hartley, and to Blyth the following year. When the company was incorporated in 1852 it adopted the name, Blyth and Tyne Railway and the tracks eventually reached Bedlington, Morpeth, Tynemouth and Monkseaton and had access to Newcastle. By 1872, when North Blyth and Newbiggin were connected, the little network reached into every corner of the coalfield, and this attracted the interest of the big North Eastern Railway, which took over the Blyth and Tyne in 1874. In 1923 the North Eastern became an integral part of the London and North Eastern Railway Company, which in turn was nationalised in 1947 as part of British Railways. Blyth Station was closed in 1964 under the so-called Beeching cuts, and a supermarket was later built on the site.

Blyth Station was a terminus, but it wasn't the end of the line, because the rails carried on past the passenger buildings to the docks. The bridge, seen here adorned with an advertisement for Nestle's Milk, took the tracks across the end of Turner Street, at the point where it met Regent Street. In later years the distinction between the two streets ended when Turner Street was renamed Regent Street. The picture was used as a postcard in November 1914 and the message on the back, written by a father to his son in London, is a poignant little snapshot into the lives of a family separated by the First World War. The man, who appears to have been an officer, had detrained elsewhere and ridden to Blyth on his horse. He was billeted in a farmhouse, but had been locked out and slept the previous night in a barn because he was late back after seeing all the soldiers. He asked his little boy to thank his mother for a letter he had received, but also to tell her that it was not easy to write because he had to keep near the guns.

Regent Street, Cowpen Quay, is seen here looking back toward the railway bridge in a picture used as a postcard in 1916. Sproat Street on the left no longer exists, cut off by dockside developments, but at the time of the photograph it led to the building and repair yards of the Blyth Shipbuilding and Dry Docks Company. Formed in the 1880s the company took over from predecessors that had been building ships on the site for 100 years. One of the yard's most notable vessels bore one of the Royal Navy's proudest names, HMS *Ark Royal*. She was a seaplane carrier, a highly innovative concept in 1914 when she was launched. The yard closed in 1927, was taken over under a new name, but closed again in 1930. It reopened in 1937 under the old name and continued to build ships until 1967. The large building on the right of the picture occupied a site between two streets named after those prominent 19th century political adversaries, Disraeli and Gladstone. It was a chapel built in 1868 for the Primitive Methodists, a branch of the church that broke away from the mainstream Wesleyan Methodists early in the 19th century, believing that they had strayed from the evangelical mission of the church's founder.

Central Blyth looks to be a busy, bustling, prosperous place in this picture from the late 1930s looking west from Bridge Street and encompassing some of Blyth's most significant buildings. In the distance is the Central Cinema with the tower of the Methodist Zion Church behind. The Wesleyan Methodist Chapel, with its grand frontage, protrudes from the right and just creeping into the right foreground is the Post Office. The library, formerly the Mechanics Institute is on the left and beyond that, the building that dominates the picture is Albion House, erected in 1896 as a department store for Hedley, Young & Company. Started by John Hedley in 1854 the business grew to become something of an institution in the town selling a range of goods including household furnishings, dress materials, haberdashery, hats, gloves and menswear. It is flanked on the side, facing camera, by Beaconsfield Street, where the Thomas Knight Memorial Hospital was situated and on the other side by Union Street, the location of the Wallaw Cinema, an Art Deco gem opened in November 1937 and saved as a pub in December 2013.

The co-operative store was a feature of many industrial communities and Blyth was no exception with a small society in Bebside, the Clive Industrial & Provident Society based in Bowes Street and the Blyth Central Industrial & Provident Society. The Central established itself as the largest in the area, doubling its membership through the 1890s. It had a number of stores, including the one shown here believed to be in Croft Road. The Central sourced produce through the Co-operative Wholesale Society (CWS) – a sign for the CWS Cremo Oats can be seen on the left – and hosted an exhibition of CWS food, clothing and handicrafts in 1903. The CWS also operated its own transport, including ships, and in 1905 put a new Tyne-built vessel, *New Pioneer* through her trials with a load of coal from Blyth on board. She passed with flying colours and carried on to Rouen, in France to discharge the cargo. As the co-operative movement contracted and consolidated the Blyth Co-operative Society was formed and it in turn was absorbed into larger groupings, which for Blyth meant a larger store, Northumbria House, being built in Waterloo Road in the 1960s.

The Empire Electric Picture Palace in Beaconsfield Street was opened in 1911. Designed by architects Henry Gibson and Pascal J. Stienlet it did not have a conventional overhanging balcony, but instead had raised, tiered rear seating. Equipped with British Talking Pictures sound system by 1929, it was taken over in 1935 by Newcastle-based cinema entrepreneur Solomon (Solly) Sheckman. Born into a poor family that had originally come from Poland, he became one of the most significant entertainment industry entrepreneurs in Britain. He bought his first cinema in Sunderland when he was just fifteen years old and at one time owned nearly 200 cinemas and halls around the country. A couple of years after acquiring the Empire, he demolished it and on the site built the 1700 seat Art Deco styled Essoldo Cinema, one of a chain of cinemas with the same name. Solly Sheckman also owned the Theatre Royal for a time and opened the Roxy Cinema in 1955. In common with many other cinemas it closed in 1964 and became a bingo hall.

To anyone who thinks about the name of the street they are on, Bridge Street must be a puzzle because there is no obvious evidence of a bridge. There was one that formerly carried the road over a tidal stream known as The Gut, but in the 1890s the stream was confined in a culvert and built over, and the bridge was consigned to history. Bridge Street is seen here looking east in a picture from the 1920s. In the right foreground are the windows of Hedley, Young & Company's store, with some of the fine draperies on display. Beyond Hedley's is a building which became the public library in 1929, but was erected as the Mechanics Institute in 1881/82. As the institute it fulfilled the function of a library and reading room, but also accommodated the offices of the Local Board on the ground floor and on the upper floor had some classrooms and a large hall for meetings and social gatherings. Further down the right hand side of the street is the Presbyterian Church. It was built in 1863 but ceased to be used for worship in the 1940s and became a factory for a while before being replaced on the site by the somewhat intrusive Bridge House.

The War Memorial is a familiar sight in towns and villages throughout the United Kingdom, but the one in this picture, at the junction of Freehold Street and Bridge Street, was not erected to commemorate the fallen from either the First or Second World Wars, but from the South African, or Boer, War of 1899 – 1902. One of the first regiments into the fight was the Northumberland Fusiliers, with the 1st and 2nd Battalions landing in different locations, within a month of each other and fighting with distinction in some of the major battles including Belmont, Modder River, Magersfontein and Nooitgedacht. With the regular army hard pressed to overcome an elusive enemy, the government called for volunteers from home defence units and six companies of what was known as the Imperial Yeomanry were raised in Northumberland. The county's involvement was therefore significant, as was the loss of life, injury and illness, facts reflected in the Blyth memorial. It was moved to Ridley Park in 1950 to sit alongside the memorials for the First and Second World Wars. The building behind the white granite cross served as Blyth's Post Office from the 1860s to the 1890s.

The Blyth Harbour Commissioners offices were built in 1913 to the designs of Newcastle based architects James Thoburn Cackett and Robert Burns Dick. It is an elegant structure exuding a sense of solid authority, but for a long time the harbour suffered for want of such qualities. During the first half of the 19th century the harbour's fortunes were controlled by the owners of the Cowpen Collieries and although they made some improvements their interests were primarily in getting coal to market. With the development of the Blyth and Tyne Railway, shipping coal from the Tyne became a practical option and Blyth languished. Formation of the Blyth Harbour Dock and Railway Company in 1853 offered some hope, but they were unable to raise sufficient funds to carry out necessary works. With pressure from the North Eastern Railway and advice from their own consulting engineer, the company was wound up and an Act of Parliament sought to set up a Harbour Commission. It was passed in 1882 granting powers to raise the funds needed properly to manage and develop the harbour.

The police station and law courts, the building framing the picture of the Harbour Commissioners' offices on the left of the facing page is also on the left of this picture looking across what was Northumberland Street to Plessey Road. Erected on the site of the former Mechanics Institute and opened in 1896, it was designed by county architect, John Cresswell, who used the polychrome effect of red brick and white stone facings common to many of Blyth's finest buildings. It is one of the town's most imposing structures and also one of the most permanent, having been used for its designed purpose for over a century, although one original element, a tall ventilation shaft at the rear was taken down in the 1960s. On the right, Plessey Road has been cut off and Jacob Keenlyside's chandlery and store has been consigned to history, as has the practice of shopkeepers covering every inch of their exterior walls with advertising. Tucked in behind the shop, on the corner of Plessey Road and Carlton Street, is a building erected in 1893 as one of many to have served as Blyth's main post office. It has also gone.

Situated in the angle formed by Wellington Street and Plessey Road is St. Cuthbert's Parish Church. Built between 1884 and 1893 to the designs of the Newcastle based architect William Searle Hicks, it superseded a chapel of ease, which was never consecrated, but had been the place of worship for the parishioners since 1751. The old building, a simple stone-built box with a bellcote and unpretentious rectangular windows, was demolished in 1925 and replaced by the church hall. The bell, a dated keystone and some church possessions were transferred from the old building to the new, to maintain the link. This picture was probably taken in the 1920s, but some subtle changes have taken place since then. The pinnacles on the tower have all been removed after one of them was blown over in a storm in 1937, causing some damage. The tower was also modified with the addition of a clock donated in 1962 by Mr. George Colpitts and placed at the base of the central mullion between the two louvered windows.

St. Cuthbert's Church tower is in the distance framed by the houses of Ridley Avenue, seen here looking north from its junction with Park Road on the left and Park View on the right. The picture is thought to date from just before the First World War after which houses were built filling the gap and trees grew to maturity, giving the street name more meaning. The Ridley name reflects that of the family which played such an important role in the development of Blyth. Successive generations, in partnership with the White family, had an interest in a number of businesses including salt pans, a glass works and tile factory, all processes that depended on coal, and they owned and operated the mines too. The Ridleys also ran a bank for a time and were active in politics. The families were united in 1742 when Matthew Ridley married his first cousin Elizabeth White and when her father died in 1763 Matthew inherited the Blagdon Estate, acquired by the Whites in 1700. By also inheriting the baronetcy, he became Sir Matthew White Ridley Bt. and the next three baronets all had the same name. The 5th baronet served in the government as Home Secretary between 1895 and 1900, and on his retirement became the 1st Viscount Ridley of Blagdon and Blyth.

Lighthouses don't just warn mariners to stay away from danger; they are sometimes used as beacons to guide them to safety. This was the role of the Blyth High Light, which worked in conjunction with the Low Light, allowing seafarers to align their vessels for the tricky approach to the harbour entrance. The 35 feet high lower part of the tower was erected in the 1780s, but as the town and docks developed around it the light was heightened in 1888 by fourteen feet and a dozen years later by another twelve feet, six inches. These later additions were built of brick with ladders to get to the top, while the original tower was stone-built with a spiral staircase inside. The tower sits behind Bath Terrace, with No. 8 having a more interesting garden ornament than most. The light was superseded in 1985 by modern navigational aids, but as a listed structure it remained in situ and with a lighthouse in an urban area Blyth has a unique curiosity. Another structure used by mariners as a navigational aid was the police station's ventilation tower and its demolition in the 1960s caused some consternation.

This house at No. 13 Bath Terrace was the home of Robert Stoker and it is possible that the picture shows the Stoker family, which is of note only because Robert's son Fred became the first secretary of the Blyth Spartans Athletic Club when it was formed in 1899 and the first meeting of the club was held in the house. Robert left Blyth soon after to pursue a career in medicine and the club later changed its name to Blyth Spartans Amateur Football Club, but the seeds of an institution that has brought fame to the town had been sown. As a non-league club playing in local competition it would have attracted little notice outside the area, but playing in the FA Cup, the Spartans have gained a fearsome reputation. The first foray beyond the opening rounds was in the 1920s, but a momentous cup run in the 1977/78 season, cemented the club's giant-killing reputation. Having disposed of league opposition in earlier rounds the club were beaten by Wrexham in a replay staged in front of a crowd of 43,000 at St. James' Park, Newcastle, instead of the club's usual home ground of Croft Park. Another famous cup-run in season 2014/15, saw the club beat Hartlepool United before succumbing to Birmingham City.

Ridley Park is a splendid recreational facility, established on ground given to the town by Sir Matthew White Ridley Bt., the 5th baronet. Bounded by streets, the docks and the railway embankment, and with one side conforming to the line of an old rope works, it was opened in July 1904 by Lord Ridley who was handed a golden key, with which to open the gate, by J. H. Nicholson, chairman of Blyth Council. The official party and a large crowd of people then went to the bandstand where speeches were made extolling the wonderful transformation of what one speaker described as, formerly, a 'refuse heap'. Later, when officials from Blyth and Cowpen Councils dined at the Star and Garter Hotel in Northumberland Street, another speaker expressed regret that it had proved difficult to get the water to stay in the lake. The problem appeared to have been solved by 1938 when this picture of children at play, was taken. Later, the rocky edge was replaced with less hazardous paving slabs and the pond has since been superseded by a more complex water playground.

As well as kicking up water in the pond, children were able to play on swings and things, while adults could enjoy putting, or a game of tennis or bowls, as these men are doing. Backed by the railway that served the South Blyth Staithes and South Harbour, and wearing their suits and cloth caps, the bowlers typify the game as played in industrial communities before the First World War, when the picture was taken. The green flourished in those early days, with two clubs Blyth Excelsior and the Blyth Ridley Bowls Clubs being formed, but the game had fallen on less happy times at the start of the 21st century when the abandoned pavilion was rescued from decay and turned into a small café, a faint echo from the opening day when nine ice cream vendors set up their barrows at the gate. The bandstand also fell victim to changing times, having been the centre of attention on the opening day when the Seaton Delaval Military Band entertained the crowds. In the years that followed it often resounded to the brass band music so popular in mining communities, but was taken away in the 1960s and replaced by a rose garden, a commentary, perhaps on the demise of industry and its associated social life.

If Blyth had not developed as a coal exporting port it might have become a seaside resort, because the beach is beautiful; it has also been seen as strategically important in times of war. During the First World War Blyth was vital, because coal was essential to keeping the country going, so the port had to be protected and in 1916 a series of artillery installations known as the Blyth Battery was built; the observation post can be seen in the distance in this picture. Protection of the port was also vital during the Second World War, but to that was added a greater threat from the air and the prospect of invasion, where a wide sandy beach would have been vulnerable, so new installations were added to the battery. After the war people used the abandoned structures for a variety of purposes, but in 2008 work on restoring this unique piece of wartime history began, giving Blyth a splendid heritage attraction. The recreational attractions of the beach remain and in 2009 these were enhanced with some colourful beach huts, redolent of the 1930s or 40s when the picture was probably taken.